Magic
HANDBOOK

POCKET TRICKS

JON TREMAINE

QEB Publishing

Editor: Michael Downey
Designer: Louise Downey
Illustrator: Mark Turner for
         Beehive Illustrations

Published in the United States by
QEB Publishing, Inc.
3 Wrigley, Suite A
Irvine, CA 92618

www.qed-publishing.co.uk

A CIP record for this book is available from the
Library of Congress.

ISBN 978 1 59566 853 0

Printed in the United States

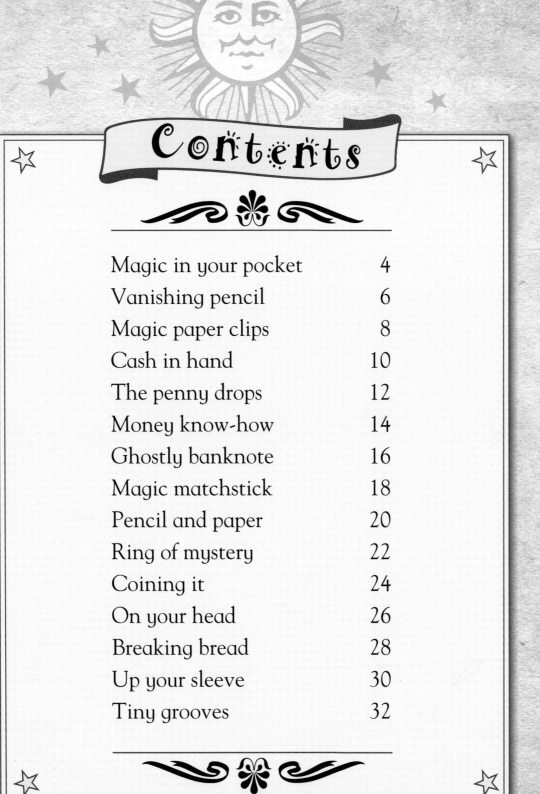

Contents

Magic in your pocket

A disappearing pencil, paper clips that mysteriously join together, a banknote that spins around all by itself, a matchstick that jumps about in your hand—these are fun tricks to do with simple props you can carry in your pocket. Tricks don't have to be complicated to be impressive!

① Preparation

Sometimes you will need to prepare something in advance to make a trick work.

Playing to the crowd

To be a good magician, you must practice your acting skills. This is because magic is as much about your performance as it is about the tricks. Always try to get your audience involved as much as possible. For example, when you do a money trick, borrow some coins or a banknote from someone in the audience.

② Difficulty rating

The tricks get harder throughout the book, so each trick has been given a rating. Two is the easiest and six is the hardest. The most difficult tricks will take a bit of practice to get right, but the results will be worth it!

Up your sleeve

Now you see it, now you don't! The vanishing key trick is a real "fooler."

Preparation

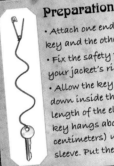

① • Attach one end of the elastic cord to the key and the other end to the safety pin.
• Fix the safety pin to the inside of your jacket's right sleeve at the top.
• Allow the key and elastic to slide down inside the sleeve. Adjust the length of the elastic so that the key hangs about an inch (three centimeters) up from the end of the sleeve. Put the jacket on.

① Just before you do this trick, reach inside your sleeve and pull the key down and grip it between your right thumb and first finger. Once you are sure that the elastic is hidden by the back of your hand, let your audience see the key.

② tha
au
pa

③ Props needed...

These are the props you will need for the tricks.

- Banknote
- Cardboard
- Coins
- Crusty bread roll
- Elastic cord
- Envelope
- Glue
- Golf tee
- Handkerchief
- Magic wand
- Matchsticks
- Metal key
- Paper
- Paper clips
- Pen
- Pencil
- Ring
- Safety pin
- Scissors
- Sticky putty
- String

④ Stages and illustrations

Step-by-step instructions, as well as illustrations, will guide you through each trick.

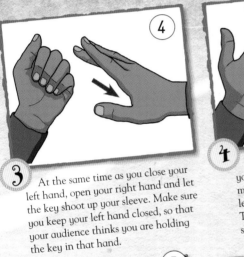

3 At the same time as you close your left hand, open your right hand and let the key shoot up your sleeve. Make sure you keep your left hand closed, so that your audience thinks you are holding the key in that hand.

4 After you show the audience that your right hand is empty, pick up your magic wand with that hand. Tap your left hand three times with the wand. Then slowly open up your left hand to show that the key has really gone!

⑤ Top Tip!

Hints and tips help you to perform the tricks better!

Top Tip!
Magicians call the type of prop used in this trick a "pull". You could make other items vanish in this way, such as a pen or a ring.

Dangerous act

The spectacular shows of magicians Siegfried and Roy featured wild animals, including the powerful white tiger. In 2003, things went badly wrong when Roy tripped as he was walking one of the tigers around the stage. The tiger tried to pick him up by biting the back of his neck. Roy was so badly hurt that the Siegfried and Roy shows had to close.

◄ Siegfried Fischbacher and Roy Horn on stage in Las Vegas with an enormous white tiger.

③

₂ches ong

alm so e. Let the y in the

2

31

⑥ Famous magicians and illusions

Find out who are the most exciting and skillful magicians, and what amazing feats they have performed.

Vanishing pencil

★ ★

Make a pencil disappear right through your hand. Don't worry—it doesn't hurt! Your friend will not have a clue how you did it.

Props needed...
* Pencil. If possible, borrow one from your friend

1 Stand with your friend to your left and hold out the palm of your left hand. Grip the pencil in your right hand in the writing position.

2 Tell your friend that you will make the pencil pass right through the palm of your left hand.

3 Bend your right arm at the elbow and swing the pencil up until it is level with your right ear. Bring the pencil down again and gently press the pointed end into your left palm. As you do this, count, "One."

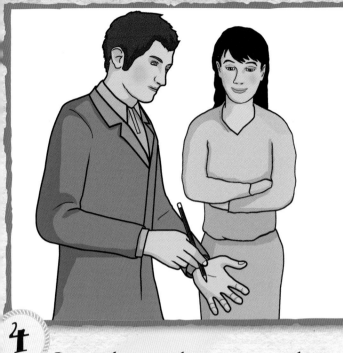

4 Swing the pencil up to your right ear again, and then down into your palm as you count, "Two."

5 Swing the pencil up to your ear a third time. This time, however, slide it behind your ear and leave it there. Bring your empty right hand down to your palm again as if you were still holding the pencil. Press your fingers into your left palm and count, "Three."

6 Show your friend that your hands are empty. The pencil has disappeared!

Top Tip!
This trick works because you keep your friend's attention on your hand. The pencil is only out of sight for a second, which is long enough for you to work your magic.

Take two simple paper clips, clip them to a banknote, and then magically link them together in the blink of an eye.

Props needed...
* Two paper clips
* Banknote. You can also use a piece of paper the same size as a banknote

1 Fold the banknote into a "Z" shape. Make sure that sections A and C are a bit longer than B, the middle section.

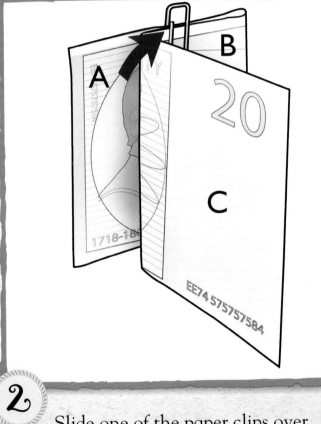

2 Slide one of the paper clips over sections A and B. Look at the drawing to make sure that you get this right.

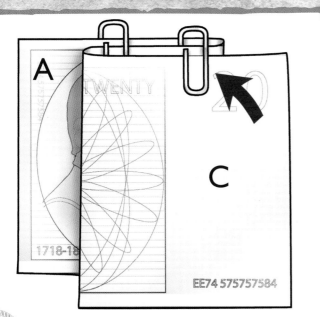

3 Now slide the second paper clip over sections B and C of the banknote.

4 Hold the end of section A in your left hand and the end of section C in your right hand. Pull these two apart with a quick, sharp pull. The two clips will link together and fly into the air.

👉 **Top Tip!**

Why not make up a story and tell it to your friend while you do the trick? It could be about a boy and a girl who meet, fall in love, and get married.

Funniest magician

Many people would agree that Tommy Cooper (1921–1984) was one of the funniest magicians ever. He was famous for wearing a fez—a red felt hat with a tassel. His tricks nearly always went wrong, and the audience laughed when he tried to put things right. He did one of his funniest tricks wearing a red cloak. From this, he pulled out lots of things, including a bucket, a beer crate, and a step-ladder!

◀ With his fez, his enormous feet, and his silly laugh, Tommy Cooper always made his audience laugh—whether his magic tricks worked or not!

Cash in hand

★ ★

You may not believe that you could get away with this simple, cheeky trick! All you have to do is make a coin vanish in your hand.

Props needed...
* Six coins

Sin Sala Bim

Harry August Jansen (1883–1955), or "Dante" as he called himself, became a full-time magician when he was just 16 years old. During a show he always said, "Sin Sala Bim" to his audience when they applauded him. No-one knows what this meant! In his most famous illusion, he pretended to saw a woman in half.

▼ Dante was one of the most gifted magicians of all time. He had a great talent for inventing magic tricks.

1 With the six coins in your right jacket pocket, say to your audience, "I will need a coin for this trick." Take all the coins out of your jacket pocket and put them on your right-hand palm.

2 With your left first finger, push one of the coins forwards a little and say "This one will do."

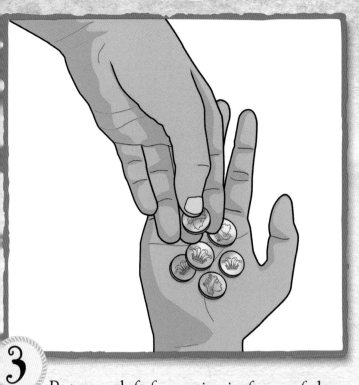

3 Put your left fingertips in front of the coin facing the audience. Your thumb is behind. Make a grabbing action as if you are picking up the coin, but do not take it away. Instead, let it drop back with the other coins.

4 Take your left hand away and close it as if it holds the coin. At the same time, put the coins in your right hand back into your pocket. When you take your hand out again, show your audience that it is empty.

5 Of course, your left hand is also empty. Your audience thinks that you have a coin in your left hand, so you must pretend to believe it, too. After about five seconds, slowly open your fingers to show your audience that the coin has really disappeared!

Top Tip!
At the end of the trick, make sure that you show your audience both of your hands. They will see that they are empty.

The penny drops

Props needed...
* Coin, which may be borrowed

Drop a coin to the ground and make it disappear! To make your audience believe that it has really vanished, you will have to practice your acting skills.

1 Hold up the coin and show it to your audience. Then pretend to drop it accidentally. Try to make the coin fall on the floor near your foot.

2 Everyone will be laughing at your clumsiness. Bend down to pick up the coin, apologizing for dropping it.

Top Tip!
If you are wearing long trousers with turnups, you could drop the coin into one of the turnups as you straighten up, rather than flipping it beneath your shoe.

3 However, instead of picking up the coin, quickly slide it under your shoe with your fingertips.

4 Make a fist with your hand, as if you have picked up the coin, and then stand up.

5 Now, you only have to open your hand and show the audience that the coin has really vanished. You should pretend to be as puzzled as your audience when you can't find the coin!

Disappearing elephant

Paul Daniels is one of the world's most successful magicians. He performs small, close-up tricks as well as huge magic illusions in the open air. These include making an elephant vanish! His wife Debbie McGee assists him in all his shows. He often saws her in half, makes her float in the air, and causes her to disappear from inside locked boxes.

◄ *Paul Daniels' most famous catchphrase is "You'll like this— not a lot, but you'll like it."*

Money know-how

Your friend will think you have special powers when you predict which coin they will choose.

Props needed...
* Four coins of different values
* Envelope
* Card that fits in the envelope
* Pen
* Glue
* Paper
* Scissors

Preparation

To show you how to do this trick, 1c, 5c, 10c, and 25c coins have been used. You can use any other four coins, but remember to change the wording on the labels.

You will think of the 5c

Point to a coin

You will think of the 1c

You will think of this coin

• On the front of the envelope, write, "You will think of the 5c."

• Take the card and, on one side, write, "Point to a coin."

• On the other side of the card, write, "You will think of the 1c."

• On a round label, write, "You will think of this coin." Glue this to the 25c coin.

• Now cut out a long, thin label and write on it, 'You will think of the 10c.' Glue this label to one side of the pen.

• Place the coins on the card with the message below facing up. The label on the 25c coin should be facing down. Slide the card into the envelope, which should be face down on the table. Put the pen on the table so that its message is also hidden.

1 Take the card out of the envelope and put it on the table so that the "Point to a coin" message is showing.

2 Slide the coins out of the envelope and arrange them on top of the card. Be careful that your friend doesn't see the label glued to the 25c coin.

3 Pick up the pen, making sure you keep the label hidden. Then say, "I want you to point to one of these coins. I already know which one you will choose. I'm thinking about it and will send you a thought message so that you choose the same one."

4 You can end this trick in one of four different ways, depending on which coin your friend chooses.

1. If the 1c coin is chosen, slide the coins off and turn over the card. The message is "You will think of the 1c."

2. If the 5c coin is chosen, ask your friend to turn over the envelope. The message is "You will think of the 5c."

3. If the 10c coin is chosen, give your friend the pen to read with the message "You will think of the 10c." Put the coins and card back into the envelope.

4. If the 25c coin is chosen, ask your friend to turn over the other coins. Then ask them to turn over the 25c with the message "You will think of this coin."

Ghostly banknote

Borrow a banknote from your friend and make it spin around in your hands. How is it done? Simple! All you need is a golf tee and some putty.

Preparation

- Ask an adult to cut off the pointed end of the golf tee with scissors, to leave about 1/2 inch (1.5 centimeters).

- Fill the hollow of the tee with the sticky putty.

Sticky putty

Press the tee onto the banknote

1 Grip the tee between the first and second fingers of your right hand. Cover the putty with your thumb. Make sure that you keep the tee hidden from your friend at all times.

2 Take your friend's banknote in your left hand and place it in your right hand. The center of the banknote should cover the putty. Press with your right thumb so that the tee sticks to the center of the underside of the banknote.

16

3 Lift off the banknote with your left hand—it should have the tee stuck to its underside.

4 Lay the note across your palms so that the tee is gripped between the edges of your palms.

Hold the tee between your palms

👉 **Top Tip!**

Finish the trick by handing the banknote back to your friend. Put the hidden tee into your pocket when your friend is not looking.

5 Keeping a gentle grip on the tee, move one of your hands slightly forward and backward. The note will begin to turn in a mysterious way. Very little movement is needed to make the banknote spin.

Magic matchstick

W atch your friend's amazed expression when you mend a broken matchstick using nothing more than a handkerchief.

Props needed...
* Handkerchief with a wide hem
* Two matchsticks

Preparation

• Look for an open corner of the handkerchief.

• Slide a matchstick into the corner until it is out of sight.

1 Lay the handkerchief on the table. The corner with the hidden matchstick should be closest to you.

2 Place the other matchstick in the center of the handkerchief so that your friend can see it.

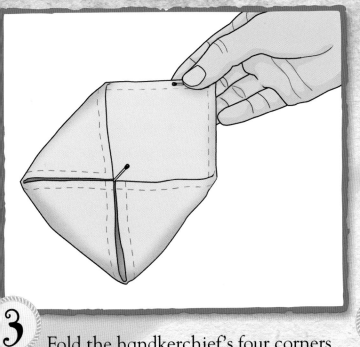

3 Fold the handkerchief's four corners to the center, taking the corner with the hidden matchstick last. Make sure you keep hold of this corner. Pick up the folded handkerchief and turn it over.

4 Ask your friend to feel if the matchstick is still there. Guide their hand to the hidden matchstick. Then ask them to hold it through the cloth and break the matchstick into as many pieces as they want.

5 Gently shake out the handkerchief. Your friend will be amazed when the unbroken matchstick falls onto the table!

☞ **Top Tip!**
When you shake the handkerchief, it is very important that you keep a good grip on the pieces of broken matchstick so that they do not fall on the table.

Pencil and paper

Balance a piece of paper on the point of a pencil and make the paper spin around and around without touching it. This looks really spooky!

Props needed...
* Sharp pencil
* Sticky putty
* Piece of paper, 2,5 x 6 inches (6 x 15 centimeters)

Preparation

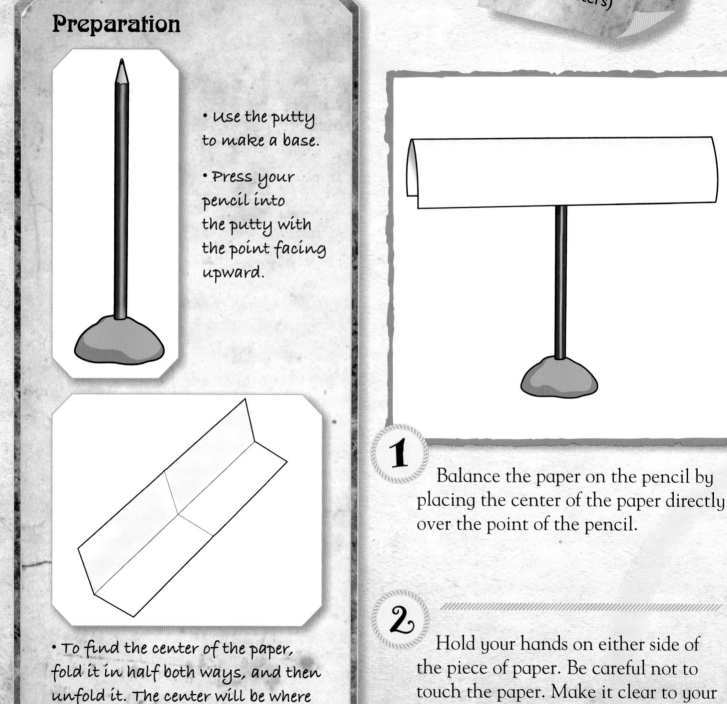

• Use the putty to make a base.

• Press your pencil into the putty with the point facing upward.

• To find the center of the paper, fold it in half both ways, and then unfold it. The center will be where the two creases cross each other.

1 Balance the paper on the pencil by placing the center of the paper directly over the point of the pencil.

2 Hold your hands on either side of the piece of paper. Be careful not to touch the paper. Make it clear to your audience that you are not blowing it.

Top Tip!

If you can't make the paper spin around, try using a thinner piece of paper. Also, make sure the point of your pencil is really sharp.

4

How does it work? Well, although there may not be a draft or breeze near you, there are still air currents in any room. Your hands block these invisible currents and cause the tiny air movements that set the paper spinning.

3

Strangely enough, you will find that the paper will start to turn. With a bit of practice, you can make it change direction. See what happens when you place your hands above the paper.

Mysterious magician

When American William Ellsworth Robinson (1861–1918) started his career as a magician, he was known as "Robinson, the Man of Mystery." Later on, he changed his name to Chung Ling Soo and pretended to be Chinese. He even wore Chinese clothes on stage. Only his best friends and other magicians knew that he was not really Chinese!

◄ To hide the fact that he was not actually Chinese, Chung Ling Soo never spoke to his audience.

CHUNG LING SOO

THE WORLD'S GREATEST CONJURER

Ring of mystery

When you remove a ring that is attached to a piece of string, your friend will be left wondering how you did it—especially as they were holding both ends of the piece of string!

Props needed...
* Piece of string, 28 inches (70 centimeters) in length
* Handkerchief
* Borrowed ring

1 Take the string and hold both of its loose ends in one hand. Pass the looped end through the borrowed ring.

2 Grip the looped end of the string and carefully bring it up and over the ring.

3 The loop you make should end up at the top of the ring. The string now looks firmly tied to the ring.

Top Tip!

You can also perform this trick using a door key with a hole at one end. Use the same method as is shown for the ring.

22

Ask your friend to hold each end of the string. Tell them to hold the string loosely so that it hangs down a bit.

Hang the handkerchief over the ring, to hide from your friend how you do your magic.

As the string is loose, you will find it easy to undo the knot. Slide the top loop down and off the ring to release the ring from the string. Bring the ring out and whip the handkerchief off at the same time. Your friend is left holding both ends of the string, now with no ring!

Coining it

Everybody knows that money doesn't grow on trees. So how about conjuring a stream of coins from a plain handkerchief?

Props needed...
* 12 coins of the same value
* Handkerchief

Preparation

• Put five coins in one pocket of your jacket and five more coins in another pocket.

• Hide the other two coins, one in each hand.

Top Tip!

This trick will show your ability with sleight of hand magic. In other words, doing something without your audience seeing what you are doing.

① Let your audience look at your handkerchief so that they can be sure there is nothing hidden in it. Take it back and lay it over your left hand. Gently nudge up the hidden coin in that hand until its shape can be seen.

②
Turn your right hand over to show the coin

Then grip the coin through the cloth with your right thumb and first finger. Turn your right hand over so that the handkerchief now falls over your right hand and the coin can be seen.

3 Take the coin away with your left hand and make it look like you are putting the coin into your left jacket pocket. What you really do, however, is hide it in your palm when you bring your left hand out again.

4 At the same time, push up the coin that you have hidden in your right hand until its shape can be seen through the handkerchief. Grip it through the cloth with your left thumb and first finger. Then toss the handkerchief over your left hand to reveal the coin.

5 Take the coin with your right hand and pretend to put it in your right pocket. This coin is then used again—remember that you already have five coins in your pockets.

6 Repeat these moves another 10 times until it looks like you have pocketed 12 coins. Empty your pockets to prove it! Remember to add the coin in each hand to the five in each pocket at the end when you empty your pockets.

On your head

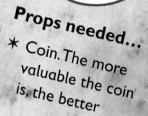

With a bit of practice, you will soon master this "now you see it, now you don't" trick. All you need is a coin and your head!

Props needed...
* Coin. The more valuable the coin is, the better

1 Ask your friend to stand in front of you with their right hand stretched out. Show them the coin in your right hand and say, "I will count to three. When I say 'Three,' I want you to grab the coin. If you get it, you can keep it."

2 Raise your right hand above your head and then bring it down again. Make sure you press the coin gently into your friend's palm when you lower it and say, "One."

▼ Popular magician Geoffrey Durham always makes his audience laugh during his shows.

Matador magic

Originally called The Great Soprendo, magician Geoffrey Durham used to dress as a matador for his magic shows. His catchphrase was "Piff, paff, poof." Then he changed his act. Now he often tours the United Kingdom with his one-man magic show, performing many famous illusions. These include sawing a woman in half!

3 Raise your hand above your head a second time and bring it down so that the coin touches your friend's palm once again. Say, "Two."

4 Repeat the move once again. But, this time, leave the coin on top of your head before you lower your hand. As you bring your hand down, say, "Three."

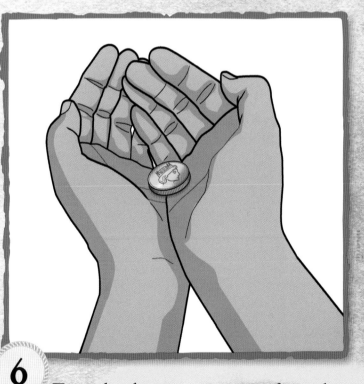

5 Your friend tries to snatch the coin, but finds that it's no longer there! Show them both your hands to prove that they are empty.

6 To make the coin reappear, first ask your friend to cup their hands and stare down at their palms. Ask them to say, "Magic money come back." Then bend over slightly so that the coin slides off your head and lands in their hands.

Breaking bread

The next time you are eating with friends and have a bread roll in your hands, why not make a coin appear out of it?

1 Hide the coin in the fingers of your right hand. Then pick up the bread roll with the same hand, so that the coin is hidden behind the roll.

2 Hold the bread roll up and look at it for a short while. Shake it by the side of your ear. Pretend that you can hear something. Then shake it by the ear of the person sitting next to you and say, "Can you hear anything? No?"

3 Shake the roll again beside your ear and pretend that you can still hear a noise. Then crack the bottom crust of the roll by pressing with your thumbs and pulling back the sides.

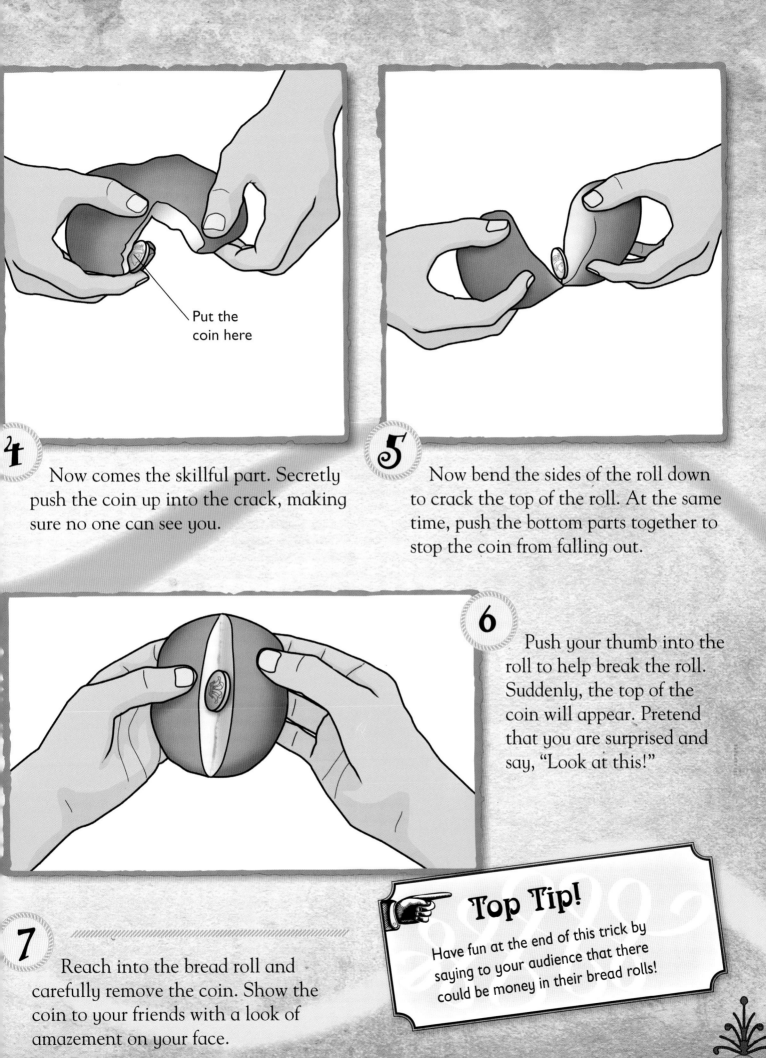

Put the
coin here

4 Now comes the skillful part. Secretly push the coin up into the crack, making sure no one can see you.

5 Now bend the sides of the roll down to crack the top of the roll. At the same time, push the bottom parts together to stop the coin from falling out.

6 Push your thumb into the roll to help break the roll. Suddenly, the top of the coin will appear. Pretend that you are surprised and say, "Look at this!"

7 Reach into the bread roll and carefully remove the coin. Show the coin to your friends with a look of amazement on your face.

Top Tip!

Have fun at the end of this trick by saying to your audience that there could be money in their bread rolls!

29

up your sleeve

Now you see it, now you don't! The vanishing key trick is a real "fooler."

Props needed...
* Metal key with a hole in it
* Elastic cord 12 inches (30 centimeters) long
* Safety pin
* Magic wand

Preparation

• Attach one end of the elastic cord to the key and the other end to the safety pin.

• Fix the safety pin to the inside of your jacket's right sleeve at the top.

• Allow the key and elastic to slide down inside the sleeve. Adjust the length of the elastic so that the key hangs about an inch (3 centimeters) up from the end of the sleeve. Put the jacket on.

1

Just before you do this trick, reach inside your sleeve and pull the key down and grip it between your right thumb and first finger. Once you are sure that the elastic is hidden by the back of your hand, let your audience see the key.

2

Hold up your left-hand palm so that it is facing the audience. Let the audience see you put the key in the palm with your right hand.

30

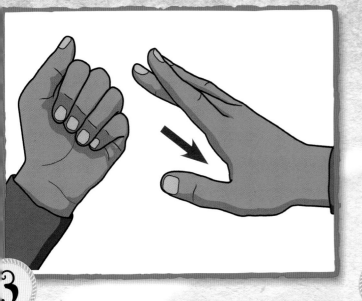

3

At the same time as you close your left hand, open your right hand and let the key shoot up your sleeve. Make sure you keep your left hand closed, so that your audience thinks you are holding the key in that hand.

4

After you show the audience that your right hand is empty, pick up your magic wand with that hand. Tap your left hand three times with the wand. Then slowly open up your left hand to show that the key has really gone!

Top Tip!

Magicians call the type of prop used in this trick a "pull." You could make other items vanish in this way, such as a pen or a ring.

Dangerous act

The spectacular shows of magicians Siegfried and Roy featured wild animals, including the powerful white tiger. In 2003, things went badly wrong when Roy tripped as he was walking one of the tigers around the stage. The tiger tried to pick him up by biting the back of his neck. Roy was so badly hurt that the Siegfried and Roy shows had to close.

◀ Siegfried Fischbacher and Roy Horn on stage in Las Vegas with an enormous white tiger.

Tiny grooves

How do you make a matchstick jump up and down by itself? Easy. Just use the invisible grooves in your fingernails!

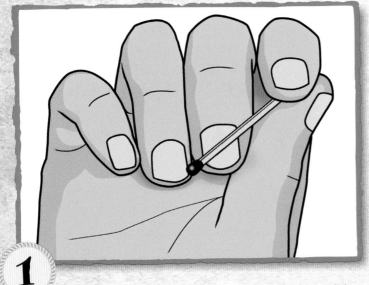

1 For this trick to work, you must hold the first matchstick in your right hand, exactly as shown. Grip the matchstick between your thumb and first finger and gently squeeze it against the nail of your second finger.

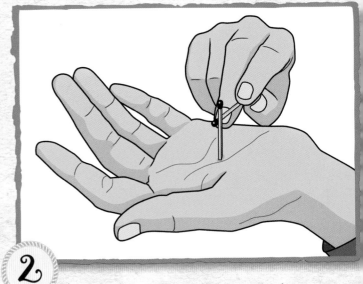

2 It is the second matchstick that jumps about. One end of this matchstick rests on the palm of your left hand. The other end sits on top of the first matchstick.

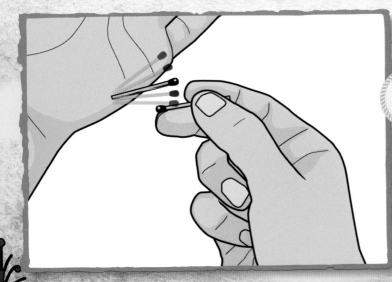

3 Squeeze the first matchstick against the nail of your second finger. This will make it skid over the tiny grooves in the nail, which causes the second matchstick to jump! If you keep pressing the first matchstick, it will skid more than 10 times before you need to adjust your grip.